FRANCIS FRITH'S

PORTHCAWL

PHOTOGRAPHIC MEMORIES

JOHN DAVID belongs to an old Porthcawl family. He is a married man with one son and two grandchildren. He served his National Service in the Royal Engineers, and he is President of the local branch of the Royal British Legion. He has been an active member of the marine rescue services all his life, and his first book dealt with the marine history of Porthcawl. His interest in local history led to the founding of the Museum and Historical Society, of which he is Chairman. For his work with local organisations, John David was awarded the MBE.

FRANCIS FRITH'S
PHOTOGRAPHIC MEMORIES

PORTHCAWL

PHOTOGRAPHIC MEMORIES

JOHN DAVID

First published in the United Kingdom in 2006 by Black Horse Books, an imprint of
The Francis Frith Collection®

Paperback Edition
ISBN 978-1-84589-514-3

Text and Design copyright The Francis Frith Collection®
Photographs copyright The Francis Frith Collection®
except where indicated.

The Frith® photographs and the Frith® logo are reproduced under licence from Heritage
Photographic Resources Ltd, the owners of the Frith® archive and trademarks.
'The Francis Frith Collection', 'Francis Frith' and 'Frith' are registered trademarks of Heritage
Photographic Resources Ltd.

All rights reserved. No photograph in this publication may be sold to a third party other than
in the original form of this publication, or framed for sale to a third party. No parts of this
publication may be reproduced, stored in a retrieval system, or transmitted, in any form, or by
any means, electronic, mechanical, photocopying, recording or otherwise, without the prior
permission of the publishers and copyright holder.

British Library Cataloguing in Publication Data

Porthcawl Photographic Memories
John David
ISBN 978-1-84589-514-3

The Francis Frith Collection
Unit 6, Oakley Business Park, Wylye Road,
Dinton, Wiltshire SP3 5EU
Tel: +44 (0) 1722 716 376
Email: info@francisfrith.co.uk
www.francisfrith.com

Printed and bound in Great Britain

Front Cover: **PORTHCAWL**, *John Street 1901*   47942t
Frontispiece: **PORTHCAWL**, *John Street 1901*   47941

The colour-tinting is for illustrative purposes only, and is not intended to be historically accurate

Aerial photographs reproduced under licence from Simmons Aerofilms Limited.
Historical Ordnance Survey maps reproduced under licence from Homecheck.co.uk

Every attempt has been made to contact copyright holders of illustrative material.
We will be happy to give full acknowledgement in future editions for any items not credited.
Any information should be directed to The Francis Frith Collection.

AS WITH ANY HISTORICAL DATABASE THE FRITH ARCHIVE IS CONSTANTLY BEING
CORRECTED AND IMPROVED AND THE PUBLISHERS WOULD WELCOME INFORMATION
ON OMISSIONS OR INACCURACIES

CONTENTS

FRANCIS FRITH: VICTORIAN PIONEER	7
PORTHCAWL - AN INTRODUCTION	10
GLAMORGANSHIRE COUNTY MAP	14
AROUND PORTHCAWL	16
ORDNANCE SURVEY MAP OF PORTHCAWL	40
PORTHCAWL FROM THE AIR	54
NOTTAGE	65
NEWTON	73
INDEX	83
Free Mounted Print Voucher	87

FRANCIS FRITH
VICTORIAN PIONEER

FRANCIS FRITH, founder of the world-famous photographic archive, was a complex and multi-talented man. A devout Quaker and a highly successful Victorian businessman, he was philosophical by nature and pioneering in outlook.

By 1855 he had already established a wholesale grocery business in Liverpool, and sold it for the astonishing sum of £200,000, which is the equivalent today of over £15,000,000. Now a very rich man, he was able to indulge his passion for travel. As a child he had pored over travel books written by early explorers, and his fancy and imagination had been stirred by family holidays to the sublime mountain regions of Wales and Scotland. 'What lands of spirit-stirring and enriching scenes and places!' he had written. He was to return to these scenes of grandeur in later years to 'recapture the thousands of vivid and tender memories', but with a different purpose. Now in his thirties, and captivated by the new science of photography, Frith set out on a series of pioneering journeys up the Nile and to the Near East that occupied him from 1856 until 1860.

INTRIGUE AND EXPLORATION

These far-flung journeys were packed with intrigue and adventure. In his life story, written when he was sixty-three, Frith tells of being held captive by bandits, and of fighting 'an awful midnight battle to the very point of surrender with a deadly pack of hungry, wild dogs'. Wearing flowing Arab costume, Frith arrived at Akaba by camel sixty years before Lawrence of Arabia, where he encountered 'desert princes and rival sheikhs, blazing with jewel-hilted swords'.

He was the first photographer to venture beyond the sixth cataract of the Nile. Africa was still the mysterious 'Dark Continent', and Stanley and Livingstone's historic meeting was a decade into the future. The conditions for picture taking confound belief. He laboured for hours in his wicker dark-room in the sweltering heat of the desert, while the volatile chemicals fizzed dangerously in their trays. Back in London he exhibited his photographs and was 'rapturously cheered' by members of the Royal Society. His reputation as a photographer was made overnight.

VENTURE OF A LIFE-TIME

Characteristically, Frith quickly spotted the opportunity to create a new business as a specialist publisher of photographs. He lived in an era of immense and sometimes violent

change. For the poor in the early part of Victoria's reign work was exhausting and the hours long, and people had precious little free time to enjoy themselves. Most had no transport other than a cart or gig at their disposal, and rarely travelled far beyond the boundaries of their own town or village. However, by the 1870s the railways had threaded their way across the country, and Bank Holidays and half-day Saturdays had been made obligatory by Act of Parliament. All of a sudden the working man and his family were able to enjoy days out and see a little more of the world.

With typical business acumen, Francis Frith foresaw that these new tourists would enjoy having souvenirs to commemorate their days out. In 1860 he married Mary Ann Rosling and set out on a new career: his aim was to photograph every city, town and village in Britain. For the next thirty years he travelled the country by train and by pony and trap, producing fine photographs of seaside resorts and beauty spots that were keenly bought by millions of Victorians. These prints were painstakingly pasted into family albums and pored over during the dark nights of winter, rekindling precious memories of summer excursions.

THE RISE OF FRITH & CO

Frith's studio was soon supplying retail shops all over the country. To meet the demand he gathered about him a small team of photographers, and published the work of independent artist-photographers of the calibre of Roger Fenton and Francis Bedford. In order to gain some understanding of the scale of Frith's business one only has to look at the catalogue issued by Frith & Co in 1886: it runs to some 670 pages, listing not only many thousands of views of the British Isles but also many photographs of most European countries, and China, Japan, the USA and Canada - note the sample page shown on page 9 from the hand-written Frith & Co ledgers recording the pictures. By 1890 Frith had created the greatest specialist photographic publishing company in the world, with over 2,000 sales outlets - more than the combined number that Boots and WH Smith have today! The picture on the next page shows the Frith & Co display board at Ingleton in the Yorkshire Dales (left of window). Beautifully constructed with a mahogany frame and gilt inserts, it could display up to a dozen local scenes.

POSTCARD BONANZA

The ever-popular holiday postcard we know today took many years to develop. In 1870 the Post Office issued the first plain cards, with a pre-printed stamp on one face. In 1894 they allowed other publishers' cards to be sent through the mail with an attached adhesive halfpenny stamp. Demand grew rapidly, and in 1895 a new size of postcard was permitted called the court card, but there was little room for illustration. In 1899, a year after Frith's death, a new card measuring 5.5 x 3.5 inches became the standard format, but it was not until 1902 that the divided back came into being, so that the address and message could be on one face and a full-size illustration on the other. Frith & Co were in the vanguard of postcard development: Frith's sons Eustace and Cyril continued their father's monumental task, expanding the number of views offered to the public and recording more and more places in Britain, as the coasts and countryside were opened up to mass travel.

Francis Frith had died in 1898 at his villa in Cannes, his great project still growing. The archive he created continued in business for another seventy years. By 1970 it contained over a third of a million pictures showing 7,000 British towns and villages.

FRANCIS FRITH'S LEGACY

Frith's legacy to us today is of immense significance and value, for the magnificent archive of evocative photographs he created provides a unique record of change in the cities, towns and villages throughout Britain over a century and more. Frith and his fellow studio photographers revisited locations many times down the years to update their views, compiling for us an enthralling and colourful pageant of British life and character.

We are fortunate that Frith was dedicated to recording the minutiae of everyday life, for it is this sheer wealth of visual data, the painstaking chronicle of changes in dress, transport, street layouts, buildings, housing, engineering and landscape that captivates us so much today. His remarkable images offer us a powerful link with the past and with the lives of our ancestors.

THE VALUE OF THE ARCHIVE TODAY

Computers have now made it possible for Frith's many thousands of images to be accessed almost instantly. Frith's images are increasingly used as visual resources, by social historians, by researchers into genealogy and ancestry, by architects and town planners, and by teachers involved in local history projects.

In addition, the archive offers every one of us an opportunity to examine the places where we and our families have lived and worked down the years. Highly successful in Frith's own era, the archive is now, a century and more on, entering a new phase of popularity. Historians consider the Francis Frith Collection to be of prime national importance. It is the only archive of its kind remaining in private ownership. Francis Frith's archive is now housed in an historic timber barn in the beautiful village of Teffont in Wiltshire. Its founder would not recognize the archive office as it is today. In place of the many thousands of dusty boxes containing glass plate negatives and an all-pervading odour of photographic chemicals, there are now ranks of computer screens. He would be amazed to watch his images travelling round the world at unimaginable speeds through internet lines.

The archive's future is both bright and exciting. Francis Frith, with his unshakeable belief in making photographs available to the greatest number of people, would undoubtedly approve of what is being done today with his lifetime's work. His photographs depicting our shared past are now bringing pleasure and enlightenment to millions around the world a century and more after his death.

PORTHCAWL
AN INTRODUCTION

PORTHCAWL is a seaside resort on the South Wales coastline of the Bristol Channel between Barry and Swansea. There are lovely coastline walks here; the Kenfig Nature Reserve lies to the north, and the Merthyr Mawr sand dunes are to the east, giving wonderful opportunities to observe the wild life – all kinds of animals, birds and plants abound. The sand dunes are amongst the highest in Europe, and the sandy beaches invite you to sit down and sun bathe and have a picnic. Sea sports are very popular, and swimming, surfing and board sailing attract visitors from far and wide. Lifeguards patrol all the beaches to give advice and assistance when required. There is a motorboat and waterski club at Newton. The harbour is busy with boats coming and going: for those who like fishing, some of the boats take out fishing parties, and

THE CHILDREN'S PADDLING POOL *c1955* P79104

in the summer months pleasure steamers run trips to resorts on the other side of the Bristol Channel. There are some very good golf courses - both links and flat courses - available in the area, and there are good hotel and boarding houses in the town.

Porthcawl is part of the parish of Newton Nottage. Traces of prehistoric tribes dating from about 2,000 BC have been found at Merthyr Mawr Warren, including a Bronze Age grave, where the body was buried in a crouched position with a beaker-type pot. Newton is a farming village. The church of St John the Baptist is 800 years old. At the start of the 16th century the small port of Newton was established, and during the 17th century a prosperous farming and seagoing community grew up around it. Goods, especially wool and woollen goods, and also limestone for fertiliser, were traded across the Bristol Channel. Nottage was also a farming community.

The name Porthcawl is first recorded in a survey of Pembroke Manor in 1628 as the small point of rocks where the breakwater is today. In 1825 work started on the construction of a small harbour here at Porthcawl Point; it opened in 1828. A horse-drawn tram brought iron and coal to the dock for shipment. The dock soon became too small, and extensive work was carried out to enlarge it - the new dock opened in 1867. A steam-powered railway brought coal from the Llynfi Valley, which was shipped to all parts of the world. All went well until 1898, when the new docks at Port Talbot and Barry opened; as they could cater for larger vessels, this meant the end for the docks at Porthcawl, which finally closed in 1906. The RNLI, who had established a lifeboat station at Porthcawl, also closed their station: it was felt that since Porthcawl harbour was no longer a working port, and little shipping traffic remained, there was no need for a lifeboat. HM Coastguard had opened a station here in

NEWTON, *The Beach c1950* N123005

1834 - they kept their station open in case any ships ran aground and the breeches buoy rescue equipment was needed. The Bristol Channel has the second highest tidal rise and fall in the world, which means that strong currents run along the coast; also the prevailing south-west wind blows onshore, which presented problems to sailing ships.

In 1894, with the change in local authorities, the parish became the Porthcawl Urban District. In 1916 the railway station was moved to a site near the harbour, and after the First World War the town developed as a holiday resort, with the inner harbour used as a swimming and boating lake. In 1920-21 the 'Figure 8' was erected on the site of the old ballast tip, and the fairground came into being. The 'Figure 8' was a large fairground ride; when you rode on it, or if seen from the air, it was in the shape of a figure 8. Camping became popular, with tents and small caravans using the dunes behind Trecco Bay. Griffin Park opened in 1934-35, containing bowling greens, a putting course, tennis courts and a children's play area.

The army, who were a source of revenue to the town, held summer camps here every year, and there was a small arms firing range in the dunes behind Newton. After the Second World War the army were considering building a permanent base here, but sadly this was not to be.

In the 1930s Mr George Pine opened an airfield at a field on the corner of Lock's Lane and the Common, and he took passengers on flights around the bay at a charge of half a crown in old money (the equivalent of 15p). Sir Alan Cobham visited the town with his flying circus, and I remember seeing an autogiro, which was an early form of helicopter. Another odd aircraft was the flying flea, a very small aeroplane. When the Second World War began, Mr Pine served in the Air Transport Command, and his plane was taken over by the RAF for training purposes.

GRIFFIN PARK *1938* 88451

The RAF opened an airfield at Stormy Down to train air gunners. One plane would tow a canvas drogue, while the trainee gunners in another plane would practice firing at the drogue. The RAF also trained bomb aimers, who practised their skills on a large wooden raft moored off Rest Bay. All this training cost many lives: there are fourteen war graves in the local cemetery where members of the British, New Zealand, Canadian and Polish air forces are buried, and also the graves of three unknown merchant sailors. The RAF also established an Air Sea Rescue base at the harbour. The personnel were billeted in Jennings Building. Their high-powered launches saved many airmen who had ditched in the Bristol Channel. The base was closed down on 31 March 1959.

After the evacuation of Dunkirk, 2,000 British soldiers were brought to Porthcawl from the south coast ports to be sorted into their different regiments. They were in a sorry state, some only partly clothed and with no equipment. About 1,000 Dutch troops also arrived, and they were camped under canvas at Newton; some of the older locals thought we had been invaded when they saw these soldiers in green uniforms and speaking in a foreign language. The beaches were planted with anti-invasion posts, short lengths of old railway line. No one was allowed on the beaches between dusk and dawn, barbed wire was placed along all the beaches in the country at high water mark, and no one was allowed to carry or use a camera. All hotels and empty houses were requisitioned by the War Office as billets for troops of all nations, and evacuees arrived from the cities to escape the bombing, including one complete school from Rochester in Kent - they used the local school for half a day, and the local children for the other half day. A number of ships were lost in the Bristol Channel, either through hitting mines or being torpedoed; the beaches became covered in wreckage and fuel oil from these sunken ships. In the lead up to the invasion of Europe in 1944, American Army engineers practised building piers on Coney Beach, and DUKS (amphibious vehicles) used to go far out to sea in all types of weather.

After the war the sand dunes at Trecco Bay were bulldozed flat and became one of the largest caravan sites in Europe, complete with all facilities such as shops, bars, a cinema, a dance hall, and a swimming pool.

In September 1963 Dr Beeching's railway cutbacks resulted in the closure of the railway line between Pyle and Porthcawl. The track was ripped up, and the station buildings were pulled down. The loss of the railway has resulted in more road traffic, but it has not stopped the holidaymakers coming to Porthcawl.

A SECTION OF A GLAMORGANSHIRE COUNTY MAP c1850
Notice that Porthcawl doesn't appear at this date

GLAMORGANSHIRE COUNTY MAP

AROUND PORTHCAWL

THE GRAND PAVILION *c1955* P79131

This fine building was opened in 1932. It cost £25,000 to build, and it has one of the finest dance floors in the country. Many married couples in South Wales first met at dances held here.

AROUND PORTHCAWL

THE LOWER PROMENADE
c1955 P79152

The Lower Promenade was built in 1934-35 at a cost of £15,000 and opened in June 1935. It is a lovely place to sit in the sun and look at the sea and chat to your friends.

THE SEAFRONT AND THE PAVILION *c1955* P79099
This view from the beach shows the Grand Pavilion and the Esplanade Hotel.

PORTHCAWL PHOTOGRAPHIC MEMORIES

ROUGH SEAS
c1960 P79249

This photograph shows rough seas breaking over the Lower Promenade, with a fine view along the Promenade: from the right we can see the Esplanade Hotel, the Grand Pavilion, the Westward Ho Hotel, and private houses, with just the corner of the Seabank Hotel on the extreme left.

CHARABANCS AND MOTORS ON THE ESPLANADE *c1926* ZZZ05638
(Courtesy of John David/Porthcawl Museum and Historical Society)

This view looks towards the harbour with the Pier Hotel on the left. A fine array of charabancs and motorcars is parked along the seafront.

AROUND PORTHCAWL

MARINE TERRACE *1901* 47940X
The ladies and their children are enjoying a stroll along the seafront beside Marine Terrace. I wonder if the children are asking for ice-creams?

THE ESPLANADE 1901 47935

This view shows the original sloping sea wall. On the far left is the Seabank Hotel in one of its early forms. During the Spanish Civil War of the 1930s, there were a number of Welsh blockade runners, and one was Mr A J Pope, who owned and lived in the Seabank Hotel. He owned three ships, 'Seabank Spray', 'Seabank' and 'Kenfig Pool'.

PORTHCAWL PHOTOGRAPHIC MEMORIES

THE ESPLANADE HOTEL *c1950*
ZZZ05642 (Courtesy of John David/Porthcawl Museum and Historical Society)

The Esplanade Hotel is seen here as many holidaymakers will remember it, as well as the many soldiers who were billeted in it during the war years. It was demolished and replaced by a modern block of flats in 2005.

THE TERRACES *1901* 47939

This is an interesting early view of the seafront. The Esplanade Hotel on the left is seen here as it was when it was built in 1887; it was designed to be easily converted into five houses if it failed as a hotel. Evans's Restaurant is to the far right.

AROUND PORTHCAWL

SEABANK HOUSE
c1860 ZZZ05627
(Courtesy of John David/
Porthcawl Museum and
Historical Society)

This very early view shows Seabank House in the mid 19th century. It later became the Seabank Hotel, seen below.

THE SEABANK HOTEL *c1955* P79117
How different the hotel looks from the way it did in ZZZ05627, above.

PORTHCAWL PHOTOGRAPHIC MEMORIES

THE BEACH *1934*
ZZZ05629 (Courtesy of John David/Porthcawl Museum and Historical Society)

This photograph was taken on 16 June 1934. It shows the new sea wall in the course of being built; it was opened in 1935 and cost £15,000.

THE LOWER PROMENADE *1938* 88457
Here we see another view of the Lower Promenade in 1938, a nice place to stroll after looking at the shops in the nearby main shopping street.

AROUND PORTHCAWL

THE COASTGUARD STATION AND THE PILOT LOOKOUT TOWER
1938 88453

These photographs show the eastern end of the Promenade, looking towards the lighthouse. The round tower, which is still there, was originally used by the ship pilots of Porthcawl as they waited for ships to signal for a pilot to bring them into dock. The building on the right was the original Coastguard Station, which was built in 1834.

THE COASTGUARD STATION AND THE PILOT LOOKOUT TOWER *c1870* ZZZ05628
(Courtesy of John David/Porthcawl Museum and Historical Society)

PORTHCAWL PHOTOGRAPHIC MEMORIES

▼ **THE FOUNTAINS** *c1955* P79120

The fountains were sited near the harbour; this is now the site of the Lifeboat Station. On the right can be seen the gas works, which used to make the town's gas supply.

▶ **THE HARBOUR** *c1875*
ZZZ05641 (Courtesy of John David/ Porthcawl Museum and Historical Society)

This is one of the earliest photographs of the new dock after the work was completed in 1867. It shows the coal hoists and also the Jennings Building, which was a warehouse and sawmill. The small building on the extreme left was the Customs House. On 5 July 1867, Robert Howell, the landlord of the Harbour Inn, fell into the old dock and was drowned. His body was recovered, and at the inquest a verdict 'found drowned' was returned. Robert was 45 years old, and left a wife and twelve children.

AROUND PORTHCAWL

◀ **THE PIER**
1901 47937

The pier and lighthouse are seen here on a calm day. On 17 August 1883 the London bark 'The William Miles', bound from Harve to Swansea in ballast, went ashore on sands to the east of Porthcawl harbour. The captain said that he had mistaken the pier light for the Mumbles light. The lifeboat the 'Chaffing Grove' was launched and took off the captain's wife and one man just before midnight. The wind increased and the 'Chaffing Grove' was relaunched, and took off the remaining 10 crew from 'The William Miles', after which the vessel was totally wrecked.

▶ **THE HARBOUR**
1960 P79205

Here we see the entrance to the harbour. The wooden posts on the right are all that remains of the two original piers. The white wooden huts on the left were used by the local air-training cadets.

PORTHCAWL PHOTOGRAPHIC MEMORIES

THE BOATING LAKE AND CONEY BEACH
c1960 P79250

This shows the harbour area and the children's boating lake. The low white building on the far side of the harbour is the Sea Cadet Base, and in the centre background is the Coney Beach Fairground.

PORTHCAWL PHOTOGRAPHIC MEMORIES

THE HARBOUR
c1880 ZZZ05640
(Courtesy of John David/
Porthcawl Museum and
Historical Society)

This view of the harbour entrance shows the wooden construction of the East Pier.

THE BREAKWATER NEARING COMPLETION c1865 ZZZ05624
(Courtesy of John David/Porthcawl Museum and Historical Society)

The extension to the breakwater is under construction in this photograph. The engineer in charge was Mr Frederick Appleby, seen here seated on the left. In October 1880 there was an accident on the breakwater in Porthcawl when a crane in which four men were working was blown into the sea by the volume of wind. One man was severely hurt and the others were rescued after nearly being drowned.

AROUND PORTHCAWL

THE RAILWAY
c1885 ZZZ05632
(Courtesy of John David/ Porthcawl Museum and Historical Society)

The inner harbour is seen in this view. The railway trucks are bringing coal from the mines in South Wales to the sailing ships waiting in the harbour; they in turn delivered coal to ports all over the world. The biggest ever shipment of coal from Porthcawl Harbour was 227,000 tons, in 1892.

AN AERIAL VIEW *c1925* ZZZ05637 (Courtesy of John David/Porthcawl Museum and Historical Society)

This aerial view shows Porthcawl Dock. From the small outer harbour (which is still there) ships went through the lock gates into the inner harbour, which had seven and a half acres of water. Beyond the harbour are the sand dunes, which were later levelled to build one of the largest caravan sites in Europe.

▶ **THE PILOT TOWER AND THE COASTGUARD STATION** *c1905*
ZZZ05631 (Courtesy of John David/Porthcawl Museum and Historical Society)

Here we have another view of the Pilot Tower and the Coastguard Station. The Coastguard Station on the right flies the White Ensign - the Coastguard service is part of the Royal Navy.

◀ **A CAPTURED GERMAN GUN SITED NEAR THE ORIGINAL COASTGUARD STATION** *c1925* ZZZ05643 (Courtesy of John David/ Porthcawl Museum and Historical Society)

This gun was captured during the First World War and was displayed close to the original coastguard station. During the Second World War the country was short of iron and steel for the manufacture of tanks, ships etc. The government held a 'scrap drive', and all iron gates, railings from houses and other objects were requisitioned, including this field gun.

AROUND PORTHCAWL

▲ THE HARBOUR 1978 ZZZ05639
(Courtesy of John David/Porthcawl Museum and Historical Society)

This view shows the entrance to the harbour in wintertime: a strong easterly wind is blowing into the dock, creating some large waves.

◄ THE HARBOUR 1954
ZZZ05635 (Courtesy of John David/Porthcawl Museum and Historical Society)

This view of the harbour shows two RAF Air Sea Rescue launches at their moorings. From the opening of the base at the outbreak of the Second World War they saved many airmen who had ditched in the Bristol Channel, and they also rescued many holidaymakers who had got into trouble off the beaches. On 31 March 1959 the RAF marine base ceased as an operational unit and the colours were lowered for the last time in Porthcawl.

PORTHCAWL PHOTOGRAPHIC MEMORIES

▼ **THE HARBOUR** *c1955* P79085
This view shows the harbour looking deserted on a winter's day.

▶ **COSY CORNER**
1960 P79206

Where the inner harbour had once been is now filled in and is used as a car park (top right). The area at the bottom of this photograph is now the site of the RNLI lifeboat station.

AROUND PORTHCAWL

◀ **COASTGUARDS AND THE 'TILLAMOOK', KENFIG BEACH**
1946 ZZZ05625
(Courtesy of John David/ Porthcawl Museum and Historical Society)

The 'Tillamook', a 10,000-ton American oil tanker, ran aground on Kenfig Beach on 1 December 1946. She had left Swansea dock in ballast and anchored off Mumbles Head. During the night she dragged her anchors and came ashore; the ship was to remain on the beach until 6 February 1947, when she was refloated. The Coastguard service set up their breeches buoy equipment in case the weather worsened and the crew had to be taken off the ship.

▶ **THE SS 'SAMTAMPA'** *1947*
ZZZ05644 (Courtesy of John David/ Porthcawl Museum and Historical Society)

A terrible tragedy took place on 23 April 1947 at Sker Point: during a severe storm the 7,000-ton SS 'Samtampa' was driven onto the rocks, where she quickly broke up into three large pieces. Rescue rockets were fired to try and rescue the crew by breeches buoy, but the wind was too strong and the lines fell short of the ship. In the meantime, the Mumbles Lifeboat had been launched. The lifeboat was later found upside down on the rocks not very far from the wrecked 'Samtampa', whose crew they had tried so very bravely to rescue. All 30 crew of the 'Samtampa' were lost, and so were the eight-strong crew of the Mumbles Lifeboat.

AROUND PORTHCAWL

THE WRECKED MUMBLES LIFEBOAT
1947 ZZZ05645 (Courtesy of John David/Porthcawl Museum and Historical Society)

Here we see the Mumbles Lifeboat as it was found, upside down on Sker Point. A service was later held here, after which the lifeboat was burnt.

PORTHCAWL PHOTOGRAPHIC MEMORIES

THE 'ALTMARK', KENFIG BEACH
1960 ZZZ05633
(Courtesy of John David/ Porthcawl Museum and Historical Society)

The MFV 'Altmark' was driven ashore in bad weather on Kenfig Beach on 12 June 1960. The one-man crew was rescued by the Coastguard Rescue Company. The ship became a total loss, and some of its timbers can still be seen sticking out of the sand.

KENFIG BEACH *1961* ZZZ05634 (Courtesy of John David/Porthcawl Museum and Historical Society)

This view shows the tug 'Cardiff' and a floating crane ashore on Kenfig Beach on 6 August 1961. Over the Bank Holiday period the crane, which was under tow, broke the tow and came ashore; the tug in trying to pass a new tow line grounded herself. They were both later towed off; the mate of the tug, who had been injured, was taken off by Coastguards using a breeches buoy.

THE PORTHCAWL LIFEBOAT CREW *2002* ZZZ05646
(Courtesy of John David/Porthcawl Museum and Historical Society)

On 26 November 2002 the Porthcawl Lifeboat was launched to go to the aid of a fishing vessel, the 'Gower Pride', which had broken down and required immediate assistance off the Nash Sands. The weather was bad - there were south-west winds of force 7 to 8, with heavy rain squalls. The lifeboat managed to tow the 'Gower Pride' out of the heavy surf on the banks and started back to Porthcawl; they were met by the Mumbles Lifeboat, which had also been launched, which towed the vessel back to Porthcawl harbour. Helmsman Aileen Jones was awarded the RNLI Bronze Medal for Gallantry, the first medal awarded to a female crew member in the history of the RNLI. Simon Ebbs was awarded the Thanks of the Institution on Vellum; Steve Knipe and Mark Buronwood were awarded Medal Service badges and certificates; and the Mumbles' Coxswain Martin Double was awarded a Letter of Appreciation.

PORTHCAWL PHOTOGRAPHIC MEMORIES

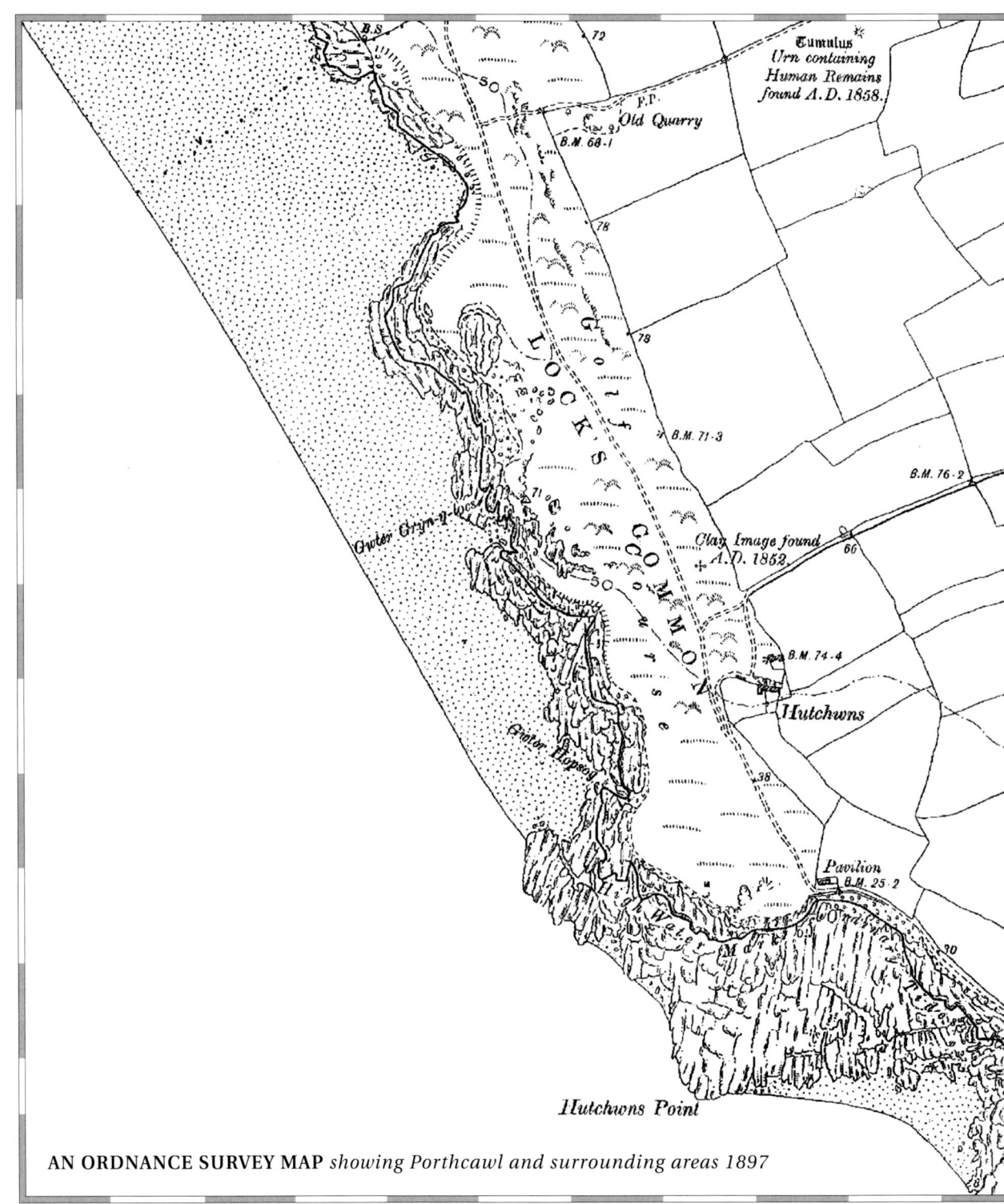

AN ORDNANCE SURVEY MAP *showing Porthcawl and surrounding areas 1897*

ORDNANCE SURVEY MAP

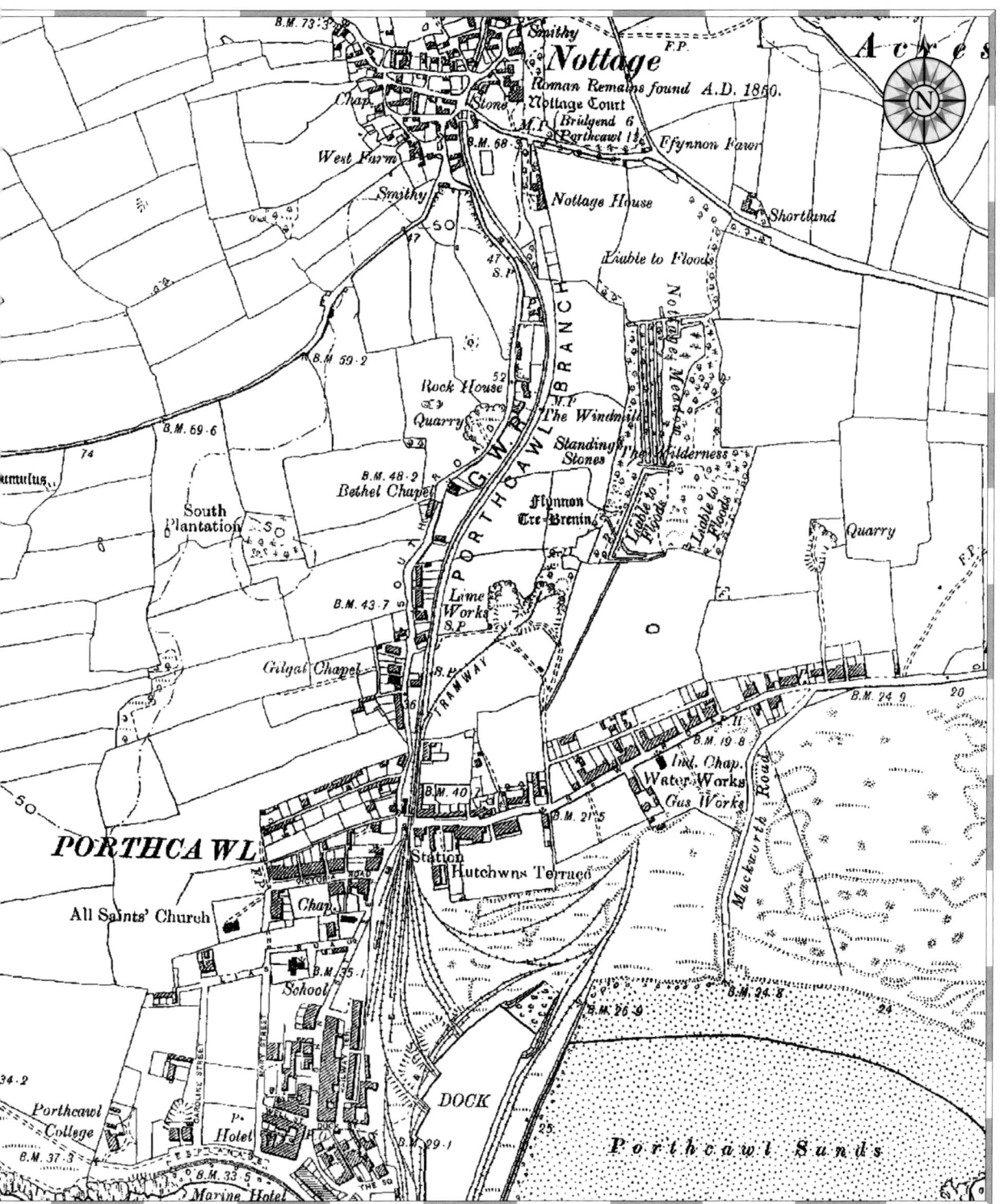

PORTHCAWL PHOTOGRAPHIC MEMORIES

▼ **THE BREAKWATER** *1998* ZZZ05647
(Courtesy of John David/Porthcawl Museum and Historical Society)

Here we see the breakwater on 4 January 1998, with waves breaking over it in a force 12 storm. During a severe storm in March 1880, the sea washed hundreds of tons of stone out of the south-east portion of the breakwater, so much so that the tide swept right through it from one side to the other, and the timber framework 'stood as if it was of open work'.

▶ **SALT LAKE** *c1925*
ZZZ05630 (Courtesy of John David/Porthcawl Museum and Historical Society)

After Porthcawl Dock closed commercially in 1906, the inner harbour was used as a boating and swimming lake. It was later decided to fill it in and develop the site; work started and was completed in the early part of the Second World War. The site is now used as a car park.

AROUND PORTHCAWL

◄ **THE MINIATURE RAILWAY** *1938*
88456

Porthcawl's miniature railway ran alongside the Eastern Promenade between the harbour and the entrance to the fairground.

▼ **JOHN STREET** *1901* 47942

On the right of this photograph is the Porthcawl Hotel with its cast iron balcony. It must be a sunny day, as the ladies on the left have their sun parasols extended and the shops have their sun-blinds down.

PORTHCAWL PHOTOGRAPHIC MEMORIES

JOHN STREET *1901* 47941

This shows the top end of John Street. The people on the right are looking in the ironmonger's shop window. A possible delivery is about to be made from the handcart in the centre of the road. Notice the fine stonework on the fronts of the buildings.

PORTHCAWL PHOTOGRAPHIC MEMORIES

JOHN STREET
c1930 ZZZ05648
(Courtesy of John David/ Porthcawl Museum and Historical Society)

Here we are looking down John Street towards the seafront. The tall building on the left was a British Restaurant during the Second World War.

JOHN STREET *1938* 88461
The site of the right of the photograph is now occupied by Woolworths; next comes the Porthcawl Hotel and Comley's Café and shop. On the left, the shop with the white-painted corner burnt down and was replaced by another shop.

AROUND PORTHCAWL

THE PORTHCAWL MUSEUM AND ART GALLERY *c1980*
ZZZ05649 (Courtesy of John David/Porthcawl Museum and Historical Society)

Here we see the entrance to the Porthcawl Museum and Art Gallery in John Street. The building was formerly the Police Station, and the museum opened in 1977. It houses a fine display of local artefacts, while the Art Society displays the work of local artists.

J HOUSE AND SONS, NEW ROAD *c1910* ZZZ05650
(Courtesy of John David/Porthcawl Museum and Historical Society)

This shows the shop of J House and Sons, established in 1877. The family firm traded until after the Second World War. What a mouth-watering display of cakes and chocolate in the shop window! The House family had another shop in the main street opposite the Coliseum Cinema. I remember as a young lad, during the war, going to the cinema with no sweets. Everything was rationed and I tried to persuade my aunt, Mrs Betty House, to let me spend my next month's ration coupons, but to no avail.

PORTHCAWL PHOTOGRAPHIC MEMORIES

▲ NEW ROAD 1901 47943

On the left of New Road was Sampson's outfitter's, draper's and grocer's shops; on the right of the photograph a sign reads 'Sampson's - ironmonger, furniture, general merchant, livery stable, horses and carriages on hire ...' They were a very busy family firm.

▶ ALL SAINTS' CHURCH c1926 ZZZ05651
(Courtesy of John David/Porthcawl Museum and Historical Society)

At the end of the 19th century, it was felt that with the opening of the dock and the growth of the town there was a need for a church in the west of the parish. The original church on this site was a corrugated iron building, consecrated on All Saints' Day 1892. In 1908 it was decided that a stone church should be built, and this church was erected and consecrated by the Bishop of Llandaff in February 1914. Porthcawl's war memorial was erected in the church grounds by the wishes of the relatives of the fallen. It bears the names of 58 local men killed in the First World War and the names of 44 local men killed in the Second World War.

AROUND PORTHCAWL

THE WESLEYAN CHAPEL *c1870*
ZZZ05626 (Courtesy of John David/Porthcawl Museum and Historical Society)

This chapel was sited on the corner of John Street and Lias Road. It was altered and extended in 1984; it was combined with Highfield Church and is now the Methodist United Reformed Church, and is named Trinity Church.

GRIFFIN PARK *1938* 88451

Gruffin Park opened in 1935. It has a putting green, bowls rink, tennis courts, and a playground for children, and in the centre the Pavilion, where you can hire sports equipment. Behind on the right was the gas works, which made the town's gas supply. The white-fronted building in the centre background is the Queen's Hotel on New Road.

PORTHCAWL PHOTOGRAPHIC MEMORIES

GRIFFIN PARK
c1955 P79071

Here we see Griffin Park in the 1950s; we are looking over the bowling greens. Behind, on New Road, the building with the lettering on the roof is the Medical Stores, advertising cameras, films and so on. The next building is the Sunny South ice-cream parlour, and then a garage.

CONEY BEACH *c1920* ZZZ05652 (Courtesy of John David/Porthcawl Museum and Historical Society)

After the dock closed, Porthcawl became a busy holiday resort. The beach is seen here full of holidaymakers enjoying the sunshine. An ice-cream cart and donkey rides are available, and there are changing huts at the top of the beach and a tearoom. Notice that the sand dunes have not yet been bulldozed flat.

AROUND PORTHCAWL

▲ **CONEY BEACH** *c1901* 47938

This view of Coney Beach shows ladies wearing long dresses, the men wearing suits and the children fully dressed - there is not a bathing costume in sight.

◄ **CONEY BEACH** *c1912* ZZZ05653
(Courtesy of John David/Porthcawl Museum and Historical Society)

The young ladies seen here by the changing huts on Coney Beach are wearing quite attractive and modest bathing costumes. There was a sign at the top of the beach which told ladies to swim on the left of the beach and men to swim on the right, and, if it was really necessary, mixed bathing was allowed in the centre of the beach.

PORTHCAWL PHOTOGRAPHIC MEMORIES

▼ **CONEY BEACH** *c1960* P79202

Here we see Coney Beach - we are looking from the Eastern Promenade.

▶ **CONEY BEACH**
1938 88454

This view shows the fairground on Coney Beach. The building on the left was an ex-First World War aircraft hanger, which has been replaced today by a modern building with bars, dining and function rooms. The helter-skelter has been replaced with a more modern fairground ride; the same also applies to the water chute on the right. One of the signs advertises 'a live giant rat, safely caged'!

AROUND PORTHCAWL

◄ **CONEY BEACH**
c1955 P79150

This view shows Coney Beach crowded with holidaymakers enjoying the sun. On 23 June 1947, hundreds of holidaymakers on Coney Beach saw the 125-ton two-masted wooden schooner 'C F H Barnstaple' run aground. The schooner had left Swansea bound for Avonmouth when she damaged her propeller on some submerged wreckage near the target buoy off Rest Bay; this caused her to make water, which poured into one of her holds. The Porthcawl Fire Brigade pumped the water out, a new propeller was fitted, and she was refloated on the flood tide.

► **THE NEW CONTINENTAL CAFÉ** *1930* 88262

Here we see the New Continental Café, a modern building overlooking the beach, with a fine view of the Bristol Channel, complete with ice-cream parlour.

PORTHCAWL PHOTOGRAPHIC MEMORIES

PORTHCAWL FROM THE AIR

PORTHCAWL *from the air 1972* AFA225897

PORTHCAWL PHOTOGRAPHIC MEMORIES

▶ **TRECCO BAY**
1938 88463

Here we see Trecco Bay; we are looking towards Newton Point, with a fine view of the sand hills before the caravan site was developed. On 7 April 1897 the 'James and Agnus', a schooner with a cargo of cement, beached at Trecco Bay after becoming badly strained bumping over the Scarweather sands. Three of the crew landed in the ship's boat and the lifeboat 'Speedwell' was launched, and saved the captain and the mate. The cargo of cement was dumped over the side, and the occasional bag of cement can still be seen at odd tides in the middle of Trecco Bay. The vessel was later refloated and taken to Appledore.

◀ **ROUGH SEAS**
c1960 P79187

In this view of the West Drive, waves from the flood tide break against the rocks.

AROUND PORTHCAWL

▲ **REST BAY** *c1955* P79103

Rest Bay is well known throughout the country as a surfing and board sailing beach, and is also a popular picnic area for families.

◄ **REST BAY** *1960* P79201

This view of Rest Bay shows the Rest Home and the Royal Porthcawl Golf Club on the right. The tide is out, and the beach is quite crowded; it is very popular with local families. The following was published in 1922 under the heading 'Aeroplane Fatality': 'The aeroplane which during the last few weeks has been visiting the prom at Porthcawl was taking passengers from Sandy Bay and Rest Bay. It belonged to Mr Williams of Neath and came to a sad end on Tuesday. The owner Mr Williams and the pilot Mr Percy Bush, both of Neath, were drowned, together with a passenger, Sgt Major Biggins of Swansea. It appears the plane nose-dived into the water, which caused an explosion. Heroic efforts were made to save the unfortunate victims, but these were unsuccessful. The machine had done a similar nose-dive on Sandy Bay a couple of weeks previously but the sands being soft broke the nose-dive impact'.

PORTHCAWL PHOTOGRAPHIC MEMORIES

THE ROYAL PORTHCAWL GOLF CLUBHOUSE
1901 47947

The eighteen-hole course of Royal Porthcawl Golf Club was opened in 1898. It is a fine links course renowned throughout the golfing world; over the years most of the top tournaments have been staged here.

THE REST COTTAGES, NEW ROAD *c1980* ZZZ05654
(Courtesy of John David/Porthcawl Museum and Historical Society)

The lease on these cottages was purchased in 1862, and this was the beginning of the Rest Convalescent Home in Porthcawl.

AROUND PORTHCAWL

THE REST HOME
c1880 ZZZ05636
(Courtesy of John David/
Porthcawl Museum and
Historical Society)

This photograph of the Rest Home was taken shortly after it opened in 1878. During the First World War it was used as a convalescent centre for sick and wounded soldiers - some 2,500 British, Australian, New Zealand and Canadian servicemen received treatment here.

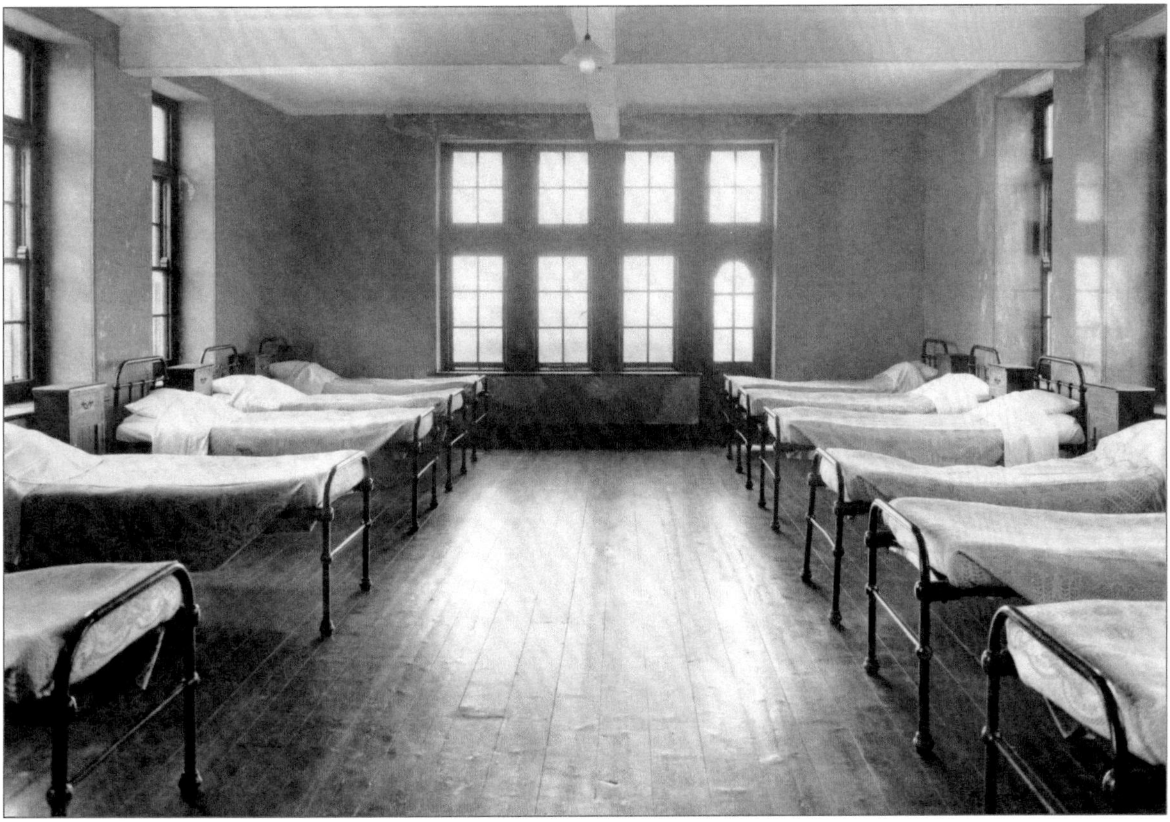

THE REST HOME, *A Ward c1935* 87710

PORTHCAWL PHOTOGRAPHIC MEMORIES

▼ **THE REST HOME,** *The Dining Room 1936* P79063

▶ **THE REST HOME**
The Dining Room c1955 P79139

AROUND PORTHCAWL

◀ **THE REST HOME**
*The Assembly Hall
1936* P79061

▶ **THE REST HOME**
The Shop 1959
P79193

THE REST SEASIDE CONVALESCENT HOME *c1955* P79172

The Rest Seaside Convalescent Home commands a wonderful view of the sandy beach and the Bristol Channel. It has been altered a lot on the inside in recent years; all facilities have been brought up to date, and new ones added.

THE REST HOME
The Paraplegic Centre 1959 P79197

In August 1941 a Spitfire crash-landed in the grounds of the Rest Convalescent Home. The pilot was left badly injured, and the Spitfire was dismantled and taken away.

SKER HOUSE *1937* 87943

Sker House was originally a grange (or outlying farm) of Neath Abbey. It has recently undergone a complete renovation and is now occupied once again.

NOTTAGE

NOTTAGE, *Nottage Court c1900* ZZZ05655
(Courtesy of John David/Porthcawl Museum and Historical Society)

Nottage Court is where Mr Richard Knight, Lord of Pembroke Manor, lives. The house dates from the Elizabethan period.

NOTTAGE
The Village 1938 88468

Nottage still looks much the same today as in this delightful old village scene. On 3 December 1940, the body of an unknown sailor was washed ashore on Newton beach. This was to be the first of four unknown sailors washed ashore during the Second World War and who are now buried at Nottage cemetery.

NOTTAGE, *The Village 1938* 88469

Here we see the Swan Inn in the centre of Nottage. The sign on the bus shelter points to the Pyle and Kenfig Golf Club, a very good local eighteen-hole links course.

NOTTAGE, *The Village Bus Shelter c1955* N124012

This view shows the village bus shelter, flanked by the Swan Inn to the left and the Farmers Arms to the right, and, on the extreme right, the stone wall of the farm buildings.

▲ **NOTTAGE,** *The Square c1955* N124010

Here we see the Square, with the village post office and general store in the centre. The building behind the car on the right is the Unitarian Church.

◀ **NOTTAGE,** *West Road c1955* N124013

This view of West Road was taken looking towards the Pyle and Kenfig Golf Course, Kenfig Pool and Kenfig Nature Reserve.

NOTTAGE, *The Well 1938* 88470
Nottage Well for many years was the main source of water for the village; the child on the right is pumping.

NOTTAGE
Cardiff Camp School c1955 N124004

Cardiff Camp School opened in 1936 for under-privileged children from Cardiff to have a summer break. Unfortunately it was closed in 1994.

NEWTON

NEWTON, *The Church c1950* N123012

The parish church of St John the Baptist at Newton is over 800 years old, and contains many interesting features. The stone pulpit dates from the 15th century; it has three panels, the centre one of which depicts the flagellation of the Saviour. The font is carved out of a solid block of sandstone, and the bowl is large enough to totally immerse a baby.

▶ NEWTON
The Church 1901 47951

On 3 June 1770 the 'Planters Welvaart', a Dutch West Indiaman of 700 tons, was driven off course in a gale and was wrecked at Porthcawl Point. 31 of her 45 crew members were saved, but amongst those drowned were three young boys, the sons of J J Jackert, who were returning home for their education. The boys were buried in Newton churchyard and the subsided gravestone was traced, restored and replaced in 2001 by the author. The beaches were strewn with the ship's cargo of sugar, coffee, cocoa, cotton etc, and the customs officer of the time had great difficulty preventing the local people from pillaging it: 'We have given constant attendance at great expense to prevent the cargo being embezzled by the country people, and to use our endeavours to save the ship, but fear that we shall do neither, as the country people are quite outrageous and threaten our lives, we seized yesterday 8 horses laden with coffee'. Behind the church to the left is the Jolly Sailor Inn.

◀ NEWTON
Beach Road c1950 N123013

Here we see the road from the church to the beach. In 1719 a report from Walter Whitney at Newton, official searcher at the port, represented that 'he is threatened, and goes in danger of his life, and having no assistant is afraid to go out at night, frightened of smugglers'.

▲ **NEWTON,** *The Village Green 1938* 88467

Newton's village green is a popular play area for youngsters. The single-storey building in the centre was once the village school, and is now used by local organisations.

◄ **NEWTON**
General View c1930
N123302

This view shows Newton from the sand dunes behind the beach. The area is now Bryneglws Gardens. On 20 March 1918, a large airship, thought to be French, sailed over Porthcawl. It sailed so low at Newton that the occupants were able to shout to some boys 'Is there any petrol here?', to which the boys replied 'Further up', meaning Porthcawl. The airship, however, made off in the direction of Port Talbot.

PORTHCAWL PHOTOGRAPHIC MEMORIES

NEWTON
The Village c1950
N123010

On the right of this photograph is Tudor Cottage, a listed building. Behind the pony and trap is Boulton's Garage.

NEWTON, *The Newton Hotel c1955* N123004

Known as the Newton Hotel at the time of this photograph, this was originally named the Ancient Briton - it was built in about 1875. It is now the Ancient Briton once more. On the right, part of the old Newton School building can be seen.

NEWTON
The Breakwater and the Lighthouse from Newton Point c1905 ZZZ05656
(Courtesy of John David/Porthcawl Museum and Historical Society)

In 1806 the naturalist and geologist William Weston Young was living in Newton. He was also an artist, and worked on the production of Nantgarw Pottery. On 16 July 1806 he signed a contract with Frederick Pigget and William Grenville to recover a cargo of copper worth £8,000 sunk in the shop 'Anne and Teresa' off Porthcawl. The wreck was two miles offshore, and lying in two fathoms of water. At an agreed price of £45 per ton plus an additional 15% from the sale of salvaged ropes and other material he made £1,400 on the transaction. He invented forceps, or grabs, which helped in this salvage business, and went on to raise 39 wrecks in the Newton area.

NEWTON, *The Ruins of the Old Red House c1910* ZZZ05657
(Courtesy of John David/Porthcawl Museum and Historical Society)

Here we see the ruins of the old Red House from Newton Point. The Red House was once known as the Weare House. It was leased in 1664 to William Lyshon, a sea-going farmer of Newton who traded between Bristol and Minehead, taking over cargos of wool, stockings and butter, then bringing back cargos for Newton, in his boat 'Five Brothers of Newton'. In the background we can see the stretch of coast from Ogmore by Sea to Nash Point.

NEWTON
A Glimpse of the Camp
c1950 N123007

Here we see the bungalows on Beach Road, with one of the army summer camps in the background.

PORTHCAWL PHOTOGRAPHIC MEMORIES

NEWTON
The Beach c1950
N123005

This view shows the beach, the sand dunes and Newton Point on the left.

NEWTON, *Beach Bungalows c1950* N123006

This view shows the beach bungalows which were built right behind the top of the beach. They were used by the military during the Second World War, but are no longer there today.

INDEX

Aerial View 31, 54-55
All Saints' Church 48
The 'Altmark', Kenfig Beach 38
Beach 24
Boating Lake and Coney Beach 28-29
Breakwater 30, 42
Breakwater Nearing Completion 30
Captured Field Gun 32
Charabancs and Motors on the Esplanade 18
Children's Paddling Pool 10
Coastguard Station & the Pilot Lookout Tower 25, 32
Coastguards and the 'Tillamook', Kenfig Beach 35
Coney Beach 50, 51, 52-53
Cosy Corner 34
Esplanade 20-21
Esplanade Hotel 22
The Fountains 26
Grand Pavilion 16
Griffin Park 12, 49, 50
Harbour 26, 27, 30, 33, 34
J House and Sons, New Road 47
John Street 43, 44-45, 46
Kenfig Beach 38
Lower Promenade 17, 24
Marine Terrace 19
Miniature Railway 43
New Continental Café 53
New Road 47, 48
Pier 27
Pilot Tower and the Coastguard Station 32
Porthcawl Lifeboat Crew 39
Porthcawl Museum and Art Gallery 47
Railway 31
Rest Bay 57
Rest Cottages 58

Rest Home 59, 60, 61, 64
Rest Seaside Convalescent Home 62-63
Rough Seas 18, 56
Royal Porthcawl Golf Clubhouse 58
Salt Lake 42
Seabank Hotel 23
Seabank House 23
Seafront and the Pavilion 17
Sker House 64
The SS 'Samtampa' 35
The Terraces 22
Trecco Bay 56
Wesleyan Chapel 49
Wrecked Mumbles Lifeboat 36-37

NOTTAGE

Cardiff Camp School 72
Nottage Court 65
The Square 71
The Village 66-67, 68-69
Village Bus Shelter 70
The Well 72
West Road 70-71

NEWTON

A Glimpse of the Camp 78-79
Beach 11, 80-81
Beach Bungalows 82
Beach Road 74
Breakwater & the Lighthouse from Newton Point 77
Church 73, 74
General View 75, 76
Newton Hotel 76
Ruins of the Old Red House 77
Village Green 75

FRITH PRODUCTS & SERVICES

Francis Frith would doubtless be pleased to know that the pioneering publishing venture he started in 1860 still continues today. Over a hundred and forty years later, The Francis Frith Collection continues in the same innovative tradition and is now one of the foremost publishers of vintage photographs in the world. Some of the current activities include:

INTERIOR DECORATION

Today Frith's photographs can be seen framed and as giant wall murals in thousands of pubs, restaurants, hotels, banks, retail stores and other public buildings throughout the country. In every case they enhance the unique local atmosphere of the places they depict and provide reminders of gentler days in an increasingly busy and frenetic world.

PRODUCT PROMOTIONS

Frith products are used by many major companies to promote the sales of their own products or to reinforce their own history and heritage. Frith promotions have been used by Hovis bread, Courage beers, Scots Porage Oats, Colman's mustard, Cadbury's foods, Mellow Birds coffee, Dunhill pipe tobacco, Guinness, and Bulmer's Cider.

GENEALOGY AND FAMILY HISTORY

As the interest in family history and roots grows world-wide, more and more people are turning to Frith's photographs of Great Britain for images of the towns, villages and streets where their ancestors lived; and, of course, photographs of the churches and chapels where their ancestors were christened, married and buried are an essential part of every genealogy tree and family album.

FRITH PRODUCTS

All Frith photographs are available Framed or just as Mounted Prints and unmounted versions. These may be ordered from the address below. Other products available are - Calendars, Jigsaws, Canvas Prints, Mugs, Tea Towels, Tableware and local and prestige books.

THE INTERNET

Over several hundred thousand Frith photographs can be viewed and purchased on the internet through the Frith websites!

For more detailed information on Frith products, look at
www.francisfrith.com

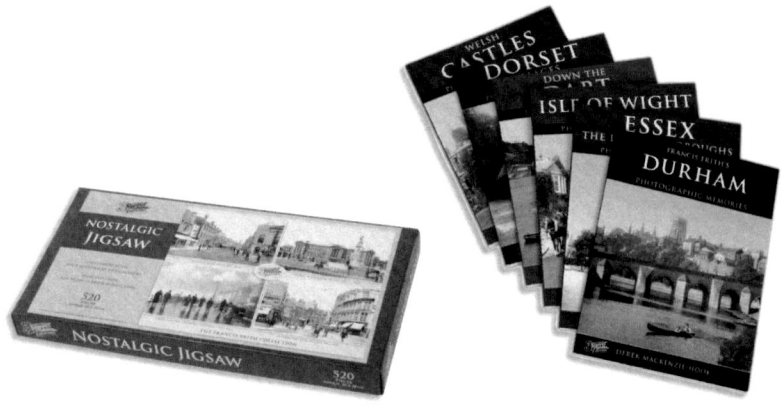
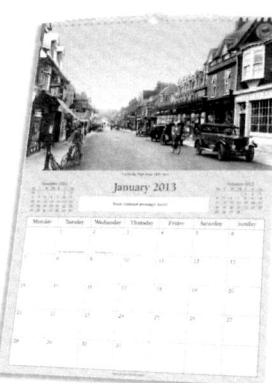

See the complete list of Frith Books at: www.francisfrith.com
This web site is regularly updated with the latest list of publications from The Francis Frith Collection. If you wish to buy books relating to another part of the country that your local bookshop does not stock, you may purchase on-line.

For further information, trade, or author enquiries please contact us at the address below:
The Francis Frith Collection, Unit 19 Kingsmead Business Park, Gillingham, Dorset SP8 5FB.
Tel: +44 (0)1722 716 376   Email: sales@francisfrith.co.uk

See Frith products on the internet at www.francisfrith.com

FREE PRINT OF YOUR CHOICE
CHOOSE A PHOTOGRAPH FROM THIS BOOK
+ POSTAGE

Mounted Print
Overall size 14 x 11 inches (355 x 280mm)

TO RECEIVE YOUR FREE PRINT

Choose any Frith photograph in this book
Simply complete the Voucher opposite and return it with your payment (to cover postage and handling) and we will print the photograph of your choice in SEPIA (size 11 x 8 inches) and supply it in a cream mount ready to frame (overall size 14 x 11 inches).

Order additional Mounted Prints at HALF PRICE - £19.00 each (normally £38.00)
If you would like to order more Frith prints from this book, possibly as gifts for friends and family, you can buy them at half price (with no additional postage costs).

Have your Mounted Prints framed
For an extra £20.00 per print you can have your mounted print(s) framed in an elegant polished wood and gilt moulding, overall size 16 x 13 inches (no additional postage required).

IMPORTANT!

❶ Please note: aerial photographs and photographs with a reference number starting with a "Z" are not Frith photographs and cannot be supplied under this offer.

❷ Offer valid for delivery to one UK address only.

❸ These special prices are only available if you use this form to order. You must use the ORIGINAL VOUCHER on this page (no copies permitted). We can only despatch to one UK address.

❹ This offer cannot be combined with any other offer.

As a customer your name & address will be stored by Frith but not sold or rented to third parties. Your data will be used for the purpose of this promotion only.

Send completed Voucher form to:
**The Francis Frith Collection,
1 Chilmark Estate House, Chilmark,
Salisbury, Wiltshire SP3 5DU**

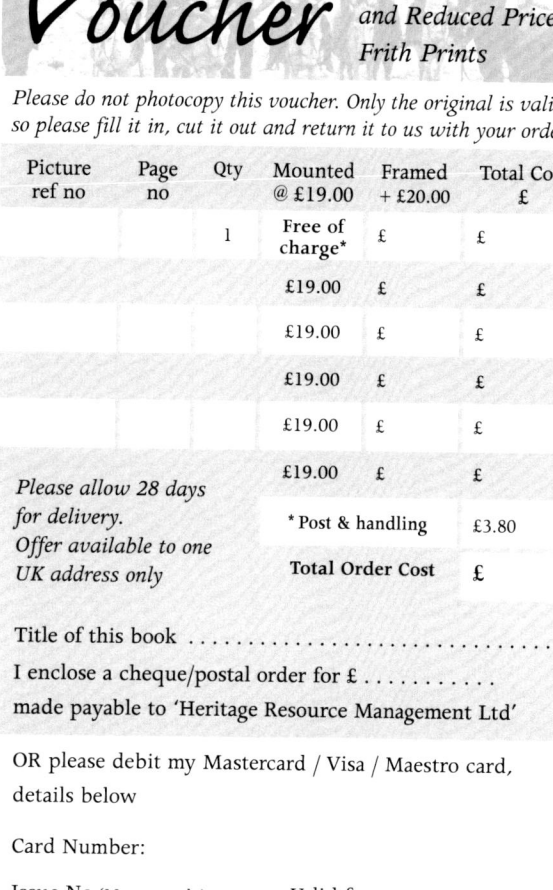

Voucher for **FREE** and Reduced Price Frith Prints

Please do not photocopy this voucher. Only the original is valid, so please fill it in, cut it out and return it to us with your order.

Picture ref no	Page no	Qty	Mounted @ £19.00	Framed + £20.00	Total Cost £
		1	Free of charge*	£	£
			£19.00	£	£
			£19.00	£	£
			£19.00	£	£
			£19.00	£	£
			£19.00	£	£

Please allow 28 days for delivery. Offer available to one UK address only

* Post & handling £3.80

Total Order Cost £

Title of this book ....

I enclose a cheque/postal order for £ ....
made payable to 'Heritage Resource Management Ltd'

OR please debit my Mastercard / Visa / Maestro card, details below

Card Number:

Issue No (Maestro only):   Valid from (Maestro):

Card Security Number: Expires:

Signature:

Name Mr/Mrs/Ms ....
Address ....
....
.... Postcode ....
Daytime Tel No ....
Email ....

Valid to 31/12/26

Can you help us with information about any of the Frith photographs in this book?

We are gradually compiling an historical record for each of the photographs in the Frith archive. It is always fascinating to find out the names of the people shown in the pictures, as well as insights into the shops, buildings and other features depicted.

If you recognize anyone in the photographs in this book, or if you have information not already included in the author's caption, do let us know. We would love to hear from you, and will try to publish it in future books or articles.

An Invitation from The Francis Frith Collection to Share Your Memories

The 'Share Your Memories' feature of our website allows members of the public to add personal memories relating to the places featured in our photographs, or comment on others already added. Seeing a place from your past can rekindle forgotten or long held memories. Why not visit the website, find photographs of places you know well and add YOUR story for others to read and enjoy? We would love to hear from you!

www.francisfrith.com/memories

Our production team

Frith books are produced by a small dedicated team at offices near Salisbury. Most have worked with the Frith Collection for many years. All have in common one quality: they have a passion for the Frith Collection.

Frith Books and Gifts

We have a wide range of books and gifts available on our website utilising our photographic archive, many of which can be individually personalised.

www.francisfrith.com